MW00395253

Bon
Appetit

Recipe Index

	Page

Recipe Index	
	Page

Recipe Index

	Page

Recipe Index	
	Page

Recipe Index

	Page

Recipe Index

	Page

Recipe Index

BON APPETIT

Recipe Name:

Servings:
Prep Time:
Cook Time:
Origin:

Instant Pot Settings	
Program:	
Mode: ☐ Less ☐ Normal ☐ High	
Time:	
Pressure Setting: ☐ High ☐ Low	
PRM: ☐ Natural ☐ Quick	Time:

Ingredients:	

Instructions

Note:

Recipe Name:

Servings:	**Instant Pot Settings**
Prep Time:	Program:
Cook Time:	Mode: ☐ Less ☐ Normal ☐ High
Origin:	Time:
	Pressure Setting: ☐ High ☐ Low
	PRM: ☐ Natural ☐ Quick / Time:

Ingredients:	

Instructions

Note:

Recipe Name:

Servings:
Prep Time:
Cook Time:
Origin:

Instant Pot Settings	
Program:	
Mode: ☐ Less ☐ Normal ☐ High	
Time:	
Pressure Setting: ☐ High ☐ Low	
PRM: ☐ Natural ☐ Quick	Time:

Ingredients:	

Instructions

Note:

Recipe Name:

Servings:	Instant Pot Settings	
Prep Time:	Program:	
Cook Time:	Mode: ☐ Less ☐ Normal ☐ High	
Origin:	Time:	
	Pressure Setting: ☐ High ☐ Low	
	PRM: ☐ Natural ☐ Quick	Time:

Ingredients:	

Instructions

Note:

Recipe Name:

Servings:
Prep Time:
Cook Time:
Origin:

Instant Pot Settings	
Program:	
Mode: ☐ Less ☐ Normal ☐ High	
Time:	
Pressure Setting: ☐ High ☐ Low	
PRM: ☐ Natural ☐ Quick	Time:

Ingredients:	

Instructions

Note:

Recipe Name:

Servings:	**Instant Pot Settings**
Prep Time:	Program:
Cook Time:	Mode: ☐ Less ☐ Normal ☐ High
Origin:	Time:
	Pressure Setting: ☐ High ☐ Low
	PRM: ☐ Natural ☐ Quick — Time:

Ingredients:	

Instructions

Note:

Recipe Name:

Servings:
Prep Time:
Cook Time:
Origin:

Instant Pot Settings	
Program:	
Mode: ☐ Less ☐ Normal ☐ High	
Time:	
Pressure Setting: ☐ High ☐ Low	
PRM: ☐ Natural ☐ Quick	Time:

Ingredients:	

Instructions

Note:

Recipe Name:

Servings:
Prep Time:
Cook Time:
Origin:

Instant Pot Settings	
Program:	
Mode: ☐ Less ☐ Normal ☐ High	
Time:	
Pressure Setting: ☐ High ☐ Low	
PRM: ☐ Natural ☐ Quick	Time:

Ingredients:	

Instructions

Note:

Recipe Name:

Servings:	Instant Pot Settings	
Prep Time:	Program:	
Cook Time:	Mode: ☐ Less ☐ Normal ☐ High	
Origin:	Time:	
	Pressure Setting: ☐ High ☐ Low	
	PRM: ☐ Natural ☐ Quick	Time:

Ingredients:	

Instructions

Note:

Recipe Name:

Servings:	Instant Pot Settings
Prep Time:	Program:
Cook Time:	Mode: ☐ Less ☐ Normal ☐ High
Origin:	Time:
	Pressure Setting: ☐ High ☐ Low
	PRM: ☐ Natural ☐ Quick / Time:

Ingredients:	

Instructions

Note:

Recipe Name:

Servings:
Prep Time:
Cook Time:
Origin:

Instant Pot Settings	
Program:	
Mode: ☐ Less ☐ Normal ☐ High	
Time:	
Pressure Setting: ☐ High ☐ Low	
PRM: ☐ Natural ☐ Quick	Time:

Ingredients:	

Instructions

Note:

Recipe Name:

Servings:	Instant Pot Settings	
Prep Time:	Program:	
Cook Time:	Mode: ☐ Less ☐ Normal ☐ High	
Origin:	Time:	
	Pressure Setting: ☐ High ☐ Low	
	PRM: ☐ Natural ☐ Quick	Time:

Ingredients:	

Instructions

Note:

Recipe Name:

Servings:
Prep Time:
Cook Time:
Origin:

Instant Pot Settings	
Program:	
Mode: ☐ Less ☐ Normal ☐ High	
Time:	
Pressure Setting: ☐ High ☐ Low	
PRM: ☐ Natural ☐ Quick	Time:

Ingredients:	

Instructions
Note:

Recipe Name:	

	Instant Pot Settings
Servings:	Program:
Prep Time:	Mode: ☐ Less ☐ Normal ☐ High
Cook Time:	Time:
Origin:	Pressure Setting: ☐ High ☐ Low
	PRM: ☐ Natural ☐ Quick	Time:

Ingredients:

Instructions

Note:

Recipe Name:

Servings:	Instant Pot Settings	
Prep Time:	Program:	
Cook Time:	Mode: ☐ Less ☐ Normal ☐ High	
Origin:	Time:	
	Pressure Setting: ☐ High ☐ Low	
	PRM: ☐ Natural ☐ Quick	Time:

Ingredients:	

Instructions
Note:

Recipe Name:

Servings:
Prep Time:
Cook Time:
Origin:

Instant Pot Settings	
Program:	
Mode: ☐ Less ☐ Normal ☐ High	
Time:	
Pressure Setting: ☐ High ☐ Low	
PRM: ☐ Natural ☐ Quick	Time:

Ingredients:	

Instructions

Note:

Recipe Name:

Servings:
Prep Time:
Cook Time:
Origin:

Instant Pot Settings	
Program:	
Mode: ☐ Less ☐ Normal ☐ High	
Time:	
Pressure Setting: ☐ High ☐ Low	
PRM: ☐ Natural ☐ Quick	Time:

Ingredients:	

Instructions

Note:

Recipe Name:

Servings:
Prep Time:
Cook Time:
Origin:

Instant Pot Settings	
Program:	
Mode: ☐ Less ☐ Normal ☐ High	
Time:	
Pressure Setting: ☐ High ☐ Low	
PRM: ☐ Natural ☐ Quick	Time:

Ingredients:	

Instructions

Note:

Recipe Name:

Servings:	**Instant Pot Settings**
Prep Time:	Program:
Cook Time:	Mode: ☐ Less ☐ Normal ☐ High
Origin:	Time:
	Pressure Setting: ☐ High ☐ Low
	PRM: ☐ Natural ☐ Quick / Time:

Ingredients:

Instructions

Note:

Recipe Name:

Servings:	**Instant Pot Settings**
Prep Time:	Program:
Cook Time:	Mode: ☐ Less ☐ Normal ☐ High
Origin:	Time:
	Pressure Setting: ☐ High ☐ Low
	PRM: ☐ Natural ☐ Quick / Time:

Ingredients:

Instructions

Note:

Recipe Name:

Servings:	Instant Pot Settings	
Prep Time:	Program:	
Cook Time:	Mode: ☐ Less ☐ Normal ☐ High	
Origin:	Time:	
	Pressure Setting: ☐ High ☐ Low	
	PRM: ☐ Natural ☐ Quick	Time:

Ingredients:	

Instructions

Note:

Recipe Name:

Servings:	Instant Pot Settings
Prep Time:	Program:
Cook Time:	Mode: ☐ Less ☐ Normal ☐ High
Origin:	Time:
	Pressure Setting: ☐ High ☐ Low
	PRM: ☐ Natural ☐ Quick / Time:

Ingredients:	

Instructions

Note:

Recipe Name:

Servings:	Instant Pot Settings	
Prep Time:	Program:	
Cook Time:	Mode: ☐ Less ☐ Normal ☐ High	
Origin:	Time:	
	Pressure Setting: ☐ High ☐ Low	
	PRM: ☐ Natural ☐ Quick	Time:

Ingredients:	

Instructions

Note:

Recipe Name:

Servings:
Prep Time:
Cook Time:
Origin:

Instant Pot Settings	
Program:	
Mode: ☐ Less ☐ Normal ☐ High	
Time:	
Pressure Setting: ☐ High ☐ Low	
PRM: ☐ Natural ☐ Quick	Time:

Ingredients:	

Instructions

Note:

Recipe Name:

Servings:	**Instant Pot Settings**
Prep Time:	Program:
Cook Time:	Mode: ☐ Less ☐ Normal ☐ High
Origin:	Time:
	Pressure Setting: ☐ High ☐ Low
	PRM: ☐ Natural ☐ Quick / Time:

Ingredients:

Instructions

Note:

Recipe Name:

Servings:	**Instant Pot Settings**
Prep Time:	Program:
Cook Time:	Mode: ☐ Less ☐ Normal ☐ High
Origin:	Time:
	Pressure Setting: ☐ High ☐ Low
	PRM: ☐ Natural ☐ Quick — Time:

Ingredients:	

Instructions

Note:

Recipe Name:

Servings:	**Instant Pot Settings**
Prep Time:	Program:
Cook Time:	Mode: ☐ Less ☐ Normal ☐ High
Origin:	Time:
	Pressure Setting: ☐ High ☐ Low
	PRM: ☐ Natural ☐ Quick — Time:

Ingredients:

Instructions

Note:

Recipe Name:

Servings:	**Instant Pot Settings**
Prep Time:	Program:
Cook Time:	Mode: ☐ Less ☐ Normal ☐ High
Origin:	Time:
	Pressure Setting: ☐ High ☐ Low
	PRM: ☐ Natural ☐ Quick — Time:

Ingredients:	

Instructions

Note:

Recipe Name:

Servings:
Prep Time:
Cook Time:
Origin:

Instant Pot Settings	
Program:	
Mode: ☐ Less ☐ Normal ☐ High	
Time:	
Pressure Setting: ☐ High ☐ Low	
PRM: ☐ Natural ☐ Quick	Time:

Ingredients:	

Instructions

Note:

Recipe Name:

Servings:	Instant Pot Settings	
Prep Time:	Program:	
Cook Time:	Mode: ☐ Less ☐ Normal ☐ High	
Origin:	Time:	
	Pressure Setting: ☐ High ☐ Low	
	PRM: ☐ Natural ☐ Quick	Time:

Ingredients:	

Instructions

Note:

Recipe Name:

Servings:
Prep Time:
Cook Time:
Origin:

Instant Pot Settings	
Program:	
Mode: ☐ Less ☐ Normal ☐ High	
Time:	
Pressure Setting: ☐ High ☐ Low	
PRM: ☐ Natural ☐ Quick	Time:

Ingredients:	

Instructions

Note:

Recipe Name:

Servings:	**Instant Pot Settings**
Prep Time:	Program:
Cook Time:	Mode: ☐ Less ☐ Normal ☐ High
Origin:	Time:
	Pressure Setting: ☐ High ☐ Low
	PRM: ☐ Natural ☐ Quick / Time:

Ingredients:

Instructions

Note:

Recipe Name:

Servings:
Prep Time:
Cook Time:
Origin:

Instant Pot Settings	
Program:	
Mode: ☐ Less ☐ Normal ☐ High	
Time:	
Pressure Setting: ☐ High ☐ Low	
PRM: ☐ Natural ☐ Quick	Time:

Ingredients:	

Instructions
Note:

Recipe Name:

Servings:	Instant Pot Settings	
Prep Time:	Program:	
Cook Time:	Mode: ☐ Less ☐ Normal ☐ High	
Origin:	Time:	
	Pressure Setting: ☐ High ☐ Low	
	PRM: ☐ Natural ☐ Quick	Time:

Ingredients:	

Instructions

Note:

Recipe Name:

Servings:
Prep Time:
Cook Time:
Origin:

Instant Pot Settings	
Program:	
Mode: ☐ Less ☐ Normal ☐ High	
Time:	
Pressure Setting: ☐ High ☐ Low	
PRM: ☐ Natural ☐ Quick	Time:

Ingredients:	

Instructions

Note:

Recipe Name:

Servings:	**Instant Pot Settings**	
Prep Time:	Program:	
Cook Time:	Mode: ☐ Less ☐ Normal ☐ High	
Origin:	Time:	
	Pressure Setting: ☐ High ☐ Low	
	PRM: ☐ Natural ☐ Quick	Time:

Ingredients:	

Instructions
Note:

Recipe Name:

Servings:
Prep Time:
Cook Time:
Origin:

Instant Pot Settings	
Program:	
Mode: ☐ Less ☐ Normal ☐ High	
Time:	
Pressure Setting: ☐ High ☐ Low	
PRM: ☐ Natural ☐ Quick	Time:

Ingredients:	

Instructions

Note:

Recipe Name:

Servings:	**Instant Pot Settings**
Prep Time:	Program:
Cook Time:	Mode: ☐ Less ☐ Normal ☐ High
Origin:	Time:
	Pressure Setting: ☐ High ☐ Low
	PRM: ☐ Natural ☐ Quick / Time:

Ingredients:	

Instructions

Note:

Recipe Name:

Servings:	Instant Pot Settings
Prep Time:	Program:
Cook Time:	Mode: ☐ Less ☐ Normal ☐ High
Origin:	Time:
	Pressure Setting: ☐ High ☐ Low
	PRM: ☐ Natural ☐ Quick — Time:

Ingredients:	

Instructions

Note:

Recipe Name:

Servings:
Prep Time:
Cook Time:
Origin:

Instant Pot Settings	
Program:	
Mode: ☐ Less ☐ Normal ☐ High	
Time:	
Pressure Setting: ☐ High ☐ Low	
PRM: ☐ Natural ☐ Quick	Time:

Ingredients:	

Instructions

Note:

Recipe Name:

Servings:
Prep Time:
Cook Time:
Origin:

Instant Pot Settings	
Program:	
Mode: ☐ Less ☐ Normal ☐ High	
Time:	
Pressure Setting: ☐ High ☐ Low	
PRM: ☐ Natural ☐ Quick	Time:

Ingredients:	

Instructions

Note:

Recipe Name:

Servings:	**Instant Pot Settings**
Prep Time:	Program:
Cook Time:	Mode: ☐ Less ☐ Normal ☐ High
Origin:	Time:
	Pressure Setting: ☐ High ☐ Low
	PRM: ☐ Natural ☐ Quick | Time:

Ingredients:	

Instructions

Note:

Recipe Name:

Servings:	Instant Pot Settings	
Prep Time:	Program:	
Cook Time:	Mode: ☐ Less ☐ Normal ☐ High	
Origin:	Time:	
	Pressure Setting: ☐ High ☐ Low	
	PRM: ☐ Natural ☐ Quick	Time:

Ingredients:	

Instructions
Note:

Recipe Name:

Servings:	**Instant Pot Settings**
Prep Time:	Program:
Cook Time:	Mode: ☐ Less ☐ Normal ☐ High
Origin:	Time:
	Pressure Setting: ☐ High ☐ Low
	PRM: ☐ Natural ☐ Quick / Time:

Ingredients:

Instructions

Note:

Recipe Name:

Servings:	Instant Pot Settings	
Prep Time:	Program:	
Cook Time:	Mode: ☐ Less ☐ Normal ☐ High	
Origin:	Time:	
	Pressure Setting: ☐ High ☐ Low	
	PRM: ☐ Natural ☐ Quick	Time:

Ingredients:	

Instructions
Note:

Recipe Name:

Servings:	Instant Pot Settings	
Prep Time:	Program:	
Cook Time:	Mode: ☐ Less ☐ Normal ☐ High	
Origin:	Time:	
	Pressure Setting: ☐ High ☐ Low	
	PRM: ☐ Natural ☐ Quick	Time:

Ingredients:	

Instructions

Note:

Recipe Name:

Servings:
Prep Time:
Cook Time:
Origin:

Instant Pot Settings	
Program:	
Mode: ☐ Less ☐ Normal ☐ High	
Time:	
Pressure Setting: ☐ High ☐ Low	
PRM: ☐ Natural ☐ Quick	Time:

Ingredients:	

Instructions

Note:

Recipe Name:

Servings:	Instant Pot Settings	
Prep Time:	Program:	
Cook Time:	Mode: ☐ Less ☐ Normal ☐ High	
Origin:	Time:	
	Pressure Setting: ☐ High ☐ Low	
	PRM: ☐ Natural ☐ Quick	Time:

Ingredients:	

Instructions

Note:

Recipe Name:

Servings:
Prep Time:
Cook Time:
Origin:

Instant Pot Settings	
Program:	
Mode: ☐ Less ☐ Normal ☐ High	
Time:	
Pressure Setting: ☐ High ☐ Low	
PRM: ☐ Natural ☐ Quick	Time:

Ingredients:	

Instructions

Note:

Recipe Name:

Servings:	**Instant Pot Settings**	
Prep Time:	Program:	
Cook Time:	Mode: ☐ Less ☐ Normal ☐ High	
Origin:	Time:	
	Pressure Setting: ☐ High ☐ Low	
	PRM: ☐ Natural ☐ Quick	Time:

Ingredients:	

Instructions

Note:

Recipe Name:

Servings:	Instant Pot Settings	
Prep Time:	Program:	
Cook Time:	Mode: ☐ Less ☐ Normal ☐ High	
Origin:	Time:	
	Pressure Setting: ☐ High ☐ Low	
	PRM: ☐ Natural ☐ Quick	Time:

Ingredients:	

Instructions

Note:

Recipe Name:

Servings:	**Instant Pot Settings**
Prep Time:	Program:
Cook Time:	Mode: ☐ Less ☐ Normal ☐ High
Origin:	Time:
	Pressure Setting: ☐ High ☐ Low
	PRM: ☐ Natural ☐ Quick — Time:

Ingredients:

Instructions

Note:

Recipe Name:

Servings:
Prep Time:
Cook Time:
Origin:

Instant Pot Settings	
Program:	
Mode: ☐ Less ☐ Normal ☐ High	
Time:	
Pressure Setting: ☐ High ☐ Low	
PRM: ☐ Natural ☐ Quick	Time:

Ingredients:	

Instructions

Note:

Recipe Name:

Servings:	Instant Pot Settings
Prep Time:	Program:
Cook Time:	Mode: ☐ Less ☐ Normal ☐ High
Origin:	Time:
	Pressure Setting: ☐ High ☐ Low
	PRM: ☐ Natural ☐ Quick / Time:

Ingredients:	

Instructions

Note:

Recipe Name:

Servings:
Prep Time:
Cook Time:
Origin:

Instant Pot Settings	
Program:	
Mode: ☐ Less ☐ Normal ☐ High	
Time:	
Pressure Setting: ☐ High ☐ Low	
PRM: ☐ Natural ☐ Quick	Time:

Ingredients:	

Instructions
Note:

Recipe Name:

Servings:
Prep Time:
Cook Time:
Origin:

Instant Pot Settings	
Program:	
Mode: ☐ Less ☐ Normal ☐ High	
Time:	
Pressure Setting: ☐ High ☐ Low	
PRM: ☐ Natural ☐ Quick	Time:

Ingredients:	

Instructions

Note:

Recipe Name:

Servings:	Instant Pot Settings	
Prep Time:	Program:	
Cook Time:	Mode: ☐ Less ☐ Normal ☐ High	
Origin:	Time:	
	Pressure Setting: ☐ High ☐ Low	
	PRM: ☐ Natural ☐ Quick	Time:

Ingredients:	

Instructions
Note:

Recipe Name:

Servings:	**Instant Pot Settings**
Prep Time:	Program:
Cook Time:	Mode: ☐ Less ☐ Normal ☐ High
Origin:	Time:
	Pressure Setting: ☐ High ☐ Low
	PRM: ☐ Natural ☐ Quick / Time:

Ingredients:

Instructions

Note:

Recipe Name:

Servings:	Instant Pot Settings	
Prep Time:	Program:	
Cook Time:	Mode: ☐ Less ☐ Normal ☐ High	
Origin:	Time:	
	Pressure Setting: ☐ High ☐ Low	
	PRM: ☐ Natural ☐ Quick	Time:

Ingredients:	

Instructions

Note:

Recipe Name:

Servings:	**Instant Pot Settings**
Prep Time:	Program:
Cook Time:	Mode: ☐ Less ☐ Normal ☐ High
Origin:	Time:
	Pressure Setting: ☐ High ☐ Low
	PRM: ☐ Natural ☐ Quick / Time:

Ingredients:

Instructions

Note:

Recipe Name:

Servings:	Instant Pot Settings	
Prep Time:	Program:	
Cook Time:	Mode: ☐ Less ☐ Normal ☐ High	
Origin:	Time:	
	Pressure Setting: ☐ High ☐ Low	
	PRM: ☐ Natural ☐ Quick	Time:

Ingredients:	

Instructions

Note:

Recipe Name:

Servings:
Prep Time:
Cook Time:
Origin:

Instant Pot Settings	
Program:	
Mode: ☐ Less ☐ Normal ☐ High	
Time:	
Pressure Setting: ☐ High ☐ Low	
PRM: ☐ Natural ☐ Quick	Time:

Ingredients:	

Instructions

Note:

Recipe Name:

Servings:
Prep Time:
Cook Time:
Origin:

Instant Pot Settings	
Program:	
Mode: ☐ Less ☐ Normal ☐ High	
Time:	
Pressure Setting: ☐ High ☐ Low	
PRM: ☐ Natural ☐ Quick	Time:

Ingredients:	

Instructions

Note:

Recipe Name:

Servings:
Prep Time:
Cook Time:
Origin:

Instant Pot Settings	
Program:	
Mode: ☐ Less ☐ Normal ☐ High	
Time:	
Pressure Setting: ☐ High ☐ Low	
PRM: ☐ Natural ☐ Quick	Time:

Ingredients:	

Instructions

Note:

Recipe Name:

Servings:	Instant Pot Settings
Prep Time:	Program:
Cook Time:	Mode: ☐ Less ☐ Normal ☐ High
Origin:	Time:
	Pressure Setting: ☐ High ☐ Low
	PRM: ☐ Natural ☐ Quick — Time:

Ingredients:	

Instructions

Note:

Recipe Name:

Servings:	**Instant Pot Settings**	
Prep Time:	Program:	
Cook Time:	Mode: ☐ Less ☐ Normal ☐ High	
Origin:	Time:	
	Pressure Setting: ☐ High ☐ Low	
	PRM: ☐ Natural ☐ Quick	Time:

Ingredients:	

Instructions

Note:

Recipe Name:

Servings:
Prep Time:
Cook Time:
Origin:

Instant Pot Settings	
Program:	
Mode: ☐ Less ☐ Normal ☐ High	
Time:	
Pressure Setting: ☐ High ☐ Low	
PRM: ☐ Natural ☐ Quick	Time:

Ingredients:	

Instructions

Note:

Recipe Name:

Servings:	Instant Pot Settings	
Prep Time:	Program:	
Cook Time:	Mode: ☐ Less ☐ Normal ☐ High	
Origin:	Time:	
	Pressure Setting: ☐ High ☐ Low	
	PRM: ☐ Natural ☐ Quick	Time:

Ingredients:	

Instructions

Note:

Recipe Name:

Servings:	**Instant Pot Settings**	
Prep Time:	Program:	
Cook Time:	Mode: ☐ Less ☐ Normal ☐ High	
Origin:	Time:	
	Pressure Setting: ☐ High ☐ Low	
	PRM: ☐ Natural ☐ Quick	Time:

Ingredients:	

Instructions

Note:

Recipe Name:

Servings:
Prep Time:
Cook Time:
Origin:

Instant Pot Settings	
Program:	
Mode: ☐ Less ☐ Normal ☐ High	
Time:	
Pressure Setting: ☐ High ☐ Low	
PRM: ☐ Natural ☐ Quick	Time:

Ingredients:	

Instructions

Note:

Recipe Name:

Servings:

Prep Time:

Cook Time:

Origin:

Instant Pot Settings

Program:

Mode: ☐ Less ☐ Normal ☐ High

Time:

Pressure Setting: ☐ High ☐ Low

PRM: ☐ Natural ☐ Quick

Time:

Ingredients:

Instructions

Note:

Recipe Name:

Servings:	**Instant Pot Settings**	
Prep Time:	Program:	
Cook Time:	Mode: ☐ Less ☐ Normal ☐ High	
Origin:	Time:	
	Pressure Setting: ☐ High ☐ Low	
	PRM: ☐ Natural ☐ Quick	Time:

Ingredients:	

Instructions

Note:

Recipe Name:

Servings:	**Instant Pot Settings**	
Prep Time:	Program:	
Cook Time:	Mode: ☐ Less ☐ Normal ☐ High	
Origin:	Time:	
	Pressure Setting: ☐ High ☐ Low	
	PRM: ☐ Natural ☐ Quick	Time:

Ingredients:	

Instructions
Note:

Recipe Name:

Servings:	Instant Pot Settings	
Prep Time:	Program:	
Cook Time:	Mode: ☐ Less ☐ Normal ☐ High	
Origin:	Time:	
	Pressure Setting: ☐ High ☐ Low	
	PRM: ☐ Natural ☐ Quick	Time:

Ingredients:	

Instructions

Note:

Recipe Name:

Servings:	**Instant Pot Settings**	
Prep Time:	Program:	
Cook Time:	Mode: ☐ Less ☐ Normal ☐ High	
Origin:	Time:	
	Pressure Setting: ☐ High ☐ Low	
	PRM: ☐ Natural ☐ Quick	Time:

Ingredients:	

Instructions

Note:

Recipe Name:

Servings:
Prep Time:
Cook Time:
Origin:

Instant Pot Settings	
Program:	
Mode: ☐ Less ☐ Normal ☐ High	
Time:	
Pressure Setting: ☐ High ☐ Low	
PRM: ☐ Natural ☐ Quick	Time:

Ingredients:	

Instructions

Note:

Recipe Name:

Servings:	Instant Pot Settings	
Prep Time:	Program:	
Cook Time:	Mode: ☐ Less ☐ Normal ☐ High	
Origin:	Time:	
	Pressure Setting: ☐ High ☐ Low	
	PRM: ☐ Natural ☐ Quick	Time:

Ingredients:	

Instructions

Note:

Recipe Name:

Servings:
Prep Time:
Cook Time:
Origin:

Instant Pot Settings	
Program:	
Mode: ☐ Less ☐ Normal ☐ High	
Time:	
Pressure Setting: ☐ High ☐ Low	
PRM: ☐ Natural ☐ Quick	Time:

Ingredients:	

Instructions

Note:

Recipe Name:

Servings:	Instant Pot Settings	
Prep Time:	Program:	
Cook Time:	Mode: ☐ Less ☐ Normal ☐ High	
Origin:	Time:	
	Pressure Setting: ☐ High ☐ Low	
	PRM: ☐ Natural ☐ Quick	Time:

Ingredients:	

Instructions

Note:

Recipe Name:

Servings:	Instant Pot Settings	
Prep Time:	Program:	
Cook Time:	Mode: ☐ Less ☐ Normal ☐ High	
Origin:	Time:	
	Pressure Setting: ☐ High ☐ Low	
	PRM: ☐ Natural ☐ Quick	Time:

Ingredients:	

Instructions

Note:

Recipe Name:

Servings:	**Instant Pot Settings**	
Prep Time:	Program:	
Cook Time:	Mode: ☐ Less ☐ Normal ☐ High	
Origin:	Time:	
	Pressure Setting: ☐ High ☐ Low	
	PRM: ☐ Natural ☐ Quick	Time:

Ingredients:	

Instructions

Note:

Recipe Name:

Servings:
Prep Time:
Cook Time:
Origin:

Instant Pot Settings	
Program:	
Mode: ☐ Less ☐ Normal ☐ High	
Time:	
Pressure Setting: ☐ High ☐ Low	
PRM: ☐ Natural ☐ Quick	Time:

Ingredients:	

Instructions

Note:

Recipe Name:

Servings:
Prep Time:
Cook Time:
Origin:

Instant Pot Settings	
Program:	
Mode: ☐ Less ☐ Normal ☐ High	
Time:	
Pressure Setting: ☐ High ☐ Low	
PRM: ☐ Natural ☐ Quick	Time:

Ingredients:	

Instructions

Note:

Recipe Name:

Servings:	**Instant Pot Settings**
Prep Time:	Program:
Cook Time:	Mode: ☐ Less ☐ Normal ☐ High
Origin:	Time:
	Pressure Setting: ☐ High ☐ Low
	PRM: ☐ Natural ☐ Quick — Time:

Ingredients:	

Instructions

Note:

Recipe Name:

Servings:	Instant Pot Settings	
Prep Time:	Program:	
Cook Time:	Mode: ☐ Less ☐ Normal ☐ High	
Origin:	Time:	
	Pressure Setting: ☐ High ☐ Low	
	PRM: ☐ Natural ☐ Quick	Time:

Ingredients:	

Instructions

Note:

Recipe Name:

Servings:	Instant Pot Settings
Prep Time:	Program:
Cook Time:	Mode: ☐ Less ☐ Normal ☐ High
Origin:	Time:
	Pressure Setting: ☐ High ☐ Low
	PRM: ☐ Natural ☐ Quick — Time:

Ingredients:	

Instructions

Note:

Recipe Name:

Servings:	Instant Pot Settings	
Prep Time:	Program:	
Cook Time:	Mode: ☐ Less ☐ Normal ☐ High	
Origin:	Time:	
	Pressure Setting: ☐ High ☐ Low	
	PRM: ☐ Natural ☐ Quick	Time:

Ingredients:	

Instructions

Note:

Recipe Name:

Servings:	Instant Pot Settings	
Prep Time:	Program:	
Cook Time:	Mode: ☐ Less ☐ Normal ☐ High	
Origin:	Time:	
	Pressure Setting: ☐ High ☐ Low	
	PRM: ☐ Natural ☐ Quick	Time:

Ingredients:	

Instructions

Note:

Recipe Name:

Servings:	Instant Pot Settings	
Prep Time:	Program:	
Cook Time:	Mode: ☐ Less ☐ Normal ☐ High	
Origin:	Time:	
	Pressure Setting: ☐ High ☐ Low	
	PRM: ☐ Natural ☐ Quick	Time:

Ingredients:	

Instructions

Note:

Recipe Name:

Servings:	Instant Pot Settings	
Prep Time:	Program:	
Cook Time:	Mode: ☐ Less ☐ Normal ☐ High	
Origin:	Time:	
	Pressure Setting: ☐ High ☐ Low	
	PRM: ☐ Natural ☐ Quick	Time:

Ingredients:	

Instructions

Note:

Recipe Name:

Servings:	Instant Pot Settings	
Prep Time:	Program:	
Cook Time:	Mode: ☐ Less ☐ Normal ☐ High	
Origin:	Time:	
	Pressure Setting: ☐ High ☐ Low	
	PRM: ☐ Natural ☐ Quick	Time:

Ingredients:	

Instructions

Note:

Recipe Name:

Servings:
Prep Time:
Cook Time:
Origin:

Instant Pot Settings	
Program:	
Mode: ☐ Less ☐ Normal ☐ High	
Time:	
Pressure Setting: ☐ High ☐ Low	
PRM: ☐ Natural ☐ Quick	Time:

Ingredients:	

Instructions

Note:

Recipe Name:

Servings:	Instant Pot Settings	
Prep Time:	Program:	
Cook Time:	Mode: ☐ Less ☐ Normal ☐ High	
Origin:	Time:	
	Pressure Setting: ☐ High ☐ Low	
	PRM: ☐ Natural ☐ Quick	Time:

Ingredients:	

Instructions

Note:

Recipe Name:

Servings:
Prep Time:
Cook Time:
Origin:

Instant Pot Settings	
Program:	
Mode: ☐ Less ☐ Normal ☐ High	
Time:	
Pressure Setting: ☐ High ☐ Low	
PRM: ☐ Natural ☐ Quick	Time:

Ingredients:	

Instructions

Note:

Recipe Name:

Servings:	Instant Pot Settings	
Prep Time:	Program:	
Cook Time:	Mode: ☐ Less ☐ Normal ☐ High	
Origin:	Time:	
	Pressure Setting: ☐ High ☐ Low	
	PRM: ☐ Natural ☐ Quick	Time:

Ingredients:	

Instructions

Note:

Recipe Name:

Servings:
Prep Time:
Cook Time:
Origin:

Instant Pot Settings	
Program:	
Mode: ☐ Less ☐ Normal ☐ High	
Time:	
Pressure Setting: ☐ High ☐ Low	
PRM: ☐ Natural ☐ Quick	Time:

Ingredients:	

Instructions

Note:

Recipe Name:

Servings:	**Instant Pot Settings**	
Prep Time:	Program:	
Cook Time:	Mode: ☐ Less ☐ Normal ☐ High	
Origin:	Time:	
	Pressure Setting: ☐ High ☐ Low	
	PRM: ☐ Natural ☐ Quick	Time:

Ingredients:	

Instructions

Note:

Recipe Name:

Servings:	**Instant Pot Settings**
Prep Time:	Program:
Cook Time:	Mode: ☐ Less ☐ Normal ☐ High
Origin:	Time:
	Pressure Setting: ☐ High ☐ Low
	PRM: ☐ Natural ☐ Quick — Time:

Ingredients:	

Instructions

Note:

Recipe Name:

Servings:
Prep Time:
Cook Time:
Origin:

Instant Pot Settings	
Program:	
Mode: ☐ Less ☐ Normal ☐ High	
Time:	
Pressure Setting: ☐ High ☐ Low	
PRM: ☐ Natural ☐ Quick	Time:

Ingredients:	

Instructions

Note:

Recipe Name:

Servings:
Prep Time:
Cook Time:
Origin:

Instant Pot Settings	
Program:	
Mode: ☐ Less ☐ Normal ☐ High	
Time:	
Pressure Setting: ☐ High ☐ Low	
PRM: ☐ Natural ☐ Quick	Time:

Ingredients:	

Instructions

Note:

Recipe Name:

Servings:	Instant Pot Settings
Prep Time:	Program:
Cook Time:	Mode: ☐ Less ☐ Normal ☐ High
Origin:	Time:
	Pressure Setting: ☐ High ☐ Low
	PRM: ☐ Natural ☐ Quick Time:

Ingredients:	

Instructions

Note:

Recipe Name:

Servings:	**Instant Pot Settings**	
Prep Time:	Program:	
Cook Time:	Mode: ☐ Less ☐ Normal ☐ High	
Origin:	Time:	
	Pressure Setting: ☐ High ☐ Low	
	PRM: ☐ Natural ☐ Quick	Time:

Ingredients:	

Instructions

Note:

Recipe Name:

Servings:	**Instant Pot Settings**
Prep Time:	Program:
Cook Time:	Mode: ☐ Less ☐ Normal ☐ High
Origin:	Time:
	Pressure Setting: ☐ High ☐ Low
	PRM: ☐ Natural ☐ Quick	Time:

Ingredients:	

Instructions

Note:

Recipe Name:

Servings:	Instant Pot Settings	
Prep Time:	Program:	
Cook Time:	Mode: ☐ Less ☐ Normal ☐ High	
Origin:	Time:	
	Pressure Setting: ☐ High ☐ Low	
	PRM: ☐ Natural ☐ Quick	Time:

Ingredients:	

Instructions

Note:

Recipe Name:

Servings:	Instant Pot Settings	
Prep Time:	Program:	
Cook Time:	Mode: ☐ Less ☐ Normal ☐ High	
Origin:	Time:	
	Pressure Setting: ☐ High ☐ Low	
	PRM: ☐ Natural ☐ Quick	Time:

Ingredients:	

Instructions

Note:

Recipe Name:

Servings:	Instant Pot Settings	
Prep Time:	Program:	
Cook Time:	Mode: ☐ Less ☐ Normal ☐ High	
Origin:	Time:	
	Pressure Setting: ☐ High ☐ Low	
	PRM: ☐ Natural ☐ Quick	Time:

Ingredients:	

Instructions

Note:

Recipe Name:

Servings:	Instant Pot Settings	
Prep Time:	Program:	
Cook Time:	Mode: ☐ Less ☐ Normal ☐ High	
Origin:	Time:	
	Pressure Setting: ☐ High ☐ Low	
	PRM: ☐ Natural ☐ Quick	Time:

Ingredients:	

Instructions

Note:

Recipe Name:

Servings:	**Instant Pot Settings**
Prep Time:	Program:
Cook Time:	Mode: ☐ Less ☐ Normal ☐ High
Origin:	Time:
	Pressure Setting: ☐ High ☐ Low
	PRM: ☐ Natural ☐ Quick — Time:

Ingredients:

Instructions

Note:

Recipe Name:

Servings:
Prep Time:
Cook Time:
Origin:

Instant Pot Settings	
Program:	
Mode: ☐ Less ☐ Normal ☐ High	
Time:	
Pressure Setting: ☐ High ☐ Low	
PRM: ☐ Natural ☐ Quick	Time:

Ingredients:	

Instructions

Note:

Recipe Name:

Servings:	**Instant Pot Settings**	
Prep Time:	Program:	
Cook Time:	Mode: ☐ Less ☐ Normal ☐ High	
Origin:	Time:	
	Pressure Setting: ☐ High ☐ Low	
	PRM: ☐ Natural ☐ Quick	Time:

Ingredients:	

Instructions

Note:

Recipe Name:

Servings:	Instant Pot Settings	
Prep Time:	Program:	
Cook Time:	Mode: ☐ Less ☐ Normal ☐ High	
Origin:	Time:	
	Pressure Setting: ☐ High ☐ Low	
	PRM: ☐ Natural ☐ Quick	Time:

Ingredients:	

Instructions

Note:

Recipe Name:

Servings:	Instant Pot Settings
Prep Time:	Program:
Cook Time:	Mode: ☐ Less ☐ Normal ☐ High
Origin:	Time:
	Pressure Setting: ☐ High ☐ Low
	PRM: ☐ Natural ☐ Quick / Time:

Ingredients:

Instructions

Note:

Recipe Name:

Servings:	**Instant Pot Settings**	
Prep Time:	Program:	
Cook Time:	Mode: ☐ Less ☐ Normal ☐ High	
Origin:	Time:	
	Pressure Setting: ☐ High ☐ Low	
	PRM: ☐ Natural ☐ Quick	Time:

Ingredients:	

Instructions

Note:

Recipe Name:

Servings:
Prep Time:
Cook Time:
Origin:

Instant Pot Settings	
Program:	
Mode: ☐ Less ☐ Normal ☐ High	
Time:	
Pressure Setting: ☐ High ☐ Low	
PRM: ☐ Natural ☐ Quick	Time:

Ingredients:	

Instructions

Note:

Recipe Name:

Servings:	Instant Pot Settings
Prep Time:	Program:
Cook Time:	Mode: ☐ Less ☐ Normal ☐ High
Origin:	Time:
	Pressure Setting: ☐ High ☐ Low
	PRM: ☐ Natural ☐ Quick — Time:

Ingredients:	

Instructions

Note:

Recipe Name:

Servings:
Prep Time:
Cook Time:
Origin:

Instant Pot Settings	
Program:	
Mode: ☐ Less ☐ Normal ☐ High	
Time:	
Pressure Setting: ☐ High ☐ Low	
PRM: ☐ Natural ☐ Quick	Time:

Ingredients:	

Instructions

Note:

Recipe Name:

Servings:	**Instant Pot Settings**	
Prep Time:	Program:	
Cook Time:	Mode: ☐ Less ☐ Normal ☐ High	
Origin:	Time:	
	Pressure Setting: ☐ High ☐ Low	
	PRM: ☐ Natural ☐ Quick	Time:

Ingredients:	

Instructions

Note:

Recipe Name:

Servings:
Prep Time:
Cook Time:
Origin:

Instant Pot Settings	
Program:	
Mode: ☐ Less ☐ Normal ☐ High	
Time:	
Pressure Setting: ☐ High ☐ Low	
PRM: ☐ Natural ☐ Quick	Time:

Ingredients:	

Instructions

Note:

Recipe Name:

Servings:	Instant Pot Settings	
Prep Time:	Program:	
Cook Time:	Mode: ☐ Less ☐ Normal ☐ High	
Origin:	Time:	
	Pressure Setting: ☐ High ☐ Low	
	PRM: ☐ Natural ☐ Quick	Time:

Ingredients:	

Instructions

Note:

Recipe Name:

Servings:	**Instant Pot Settings**	
Prep Time:	Program:	
Cook Time:	Mode: ☐ Less ☐ Normal ☐ High	
Origin:	Time:	
	Pressure Setting: ☐ High ☐ Low	
	PRM: ☐ Natural ☐ Quick	Time:

Ingredients:	

Instructions

Note:

Recipe Name:

Servings:	**Instant Pot Settings**
Prep Time:	Program:
Cook Time:	Mode: ☐ Less ☐ Normal ☐ High
Origin:	Time:
	Pressure Setting: ☐ High ☐ Low
	PRM: ☐ Natural ☐ Quick / Time:

Ingredients:	

Instructions

Note:

Recipe Name:

Servings:	**Instant Pot Settings**
Prep Time:	Program:
Cook Time:	Mode: ☐ Less ☐ Normal ☐ High
Origin:	Time:
	Pressure Setting: ☐ High ☐ Low
	PRM: ☐ Natural ☐ Quick / Time:

Ingredients:	

Instructions

Note:

Recipe Name:

Servings:	Instant Pot Settings
Prep Time:	Program:
Cook Time:	Mode: ☐ Less ☐ Normal ☐ High
Origin:	Time:
	Pressure Setting: ☐ High ☐ Low
	PRM: ☐ Natural ☐ Quick — Time:

Ingredients:

Instructions

Note:

Recipe Name:

Servings:
Prep Time:
Cook Time:
Origin:

Instant Pot Settings	
Program:	
Mode: ☐ Less ☐ Normal ☐ High	
Time:	
Pressure Setting: ☐ High ☐ Low	
PRM: ☐ Natural ☐ Quick	Time:

Ingredients:	

Instructions

Note:

Recipe Name:

Servings:	Instant Pot Settings
Prep Time:	Program:
Cook Time:	Mode: ☐ Less ☐ Normal ☐ High
Origin:	Time:
	Pressure Setting: ☐ High ☐ Low
	PRM: ☐ Natural ☐ Quick Time:

Ingredients:	

Instructions

Note:

Recipe Name:

Servings:
Prep Time:
Cook Time:
Origin:

Instant Pot Settings	
Program:	
Mode: ☐ Less ☐ Normal ☐ High	
Time:	
Pressure Setting: ☐ High ☐ Low	
PRM: ☐ Natural ☐ Quick	Time:

Ingredients:	

Instructions

Note:

Made in the USA
San Bernardino, CA
26 July 2018